The Heart of the TEACHER

Building Character Values Through Education

Christopher Calhoun '18

Dr. Mariea Calhoun Smith

Print information available on the last page

Rev. date: 10/12/2018

To order additional copies of this book, contact:
Xlibris
1-888-795-4274
www.Xlibris.com
Orders@Xlibris.com

Dedication

I would like to dedicate this book to my Lord and Savior Jesus Christ. He has given me the ability to write this book as with all the other books he has inspired me to write.

I would like to dedicate this book to a special group of ladies that requested it (Ms. Ward & Ms. Holloway). I also would like to dedicate this book to all teachers (whether in school or teaching at church).

I would like to dedicate this book to all my grandchildren (Maddie, Xavier and Lala Renae, Jah'Kari, Jak'iryn Michael Jr, Mekhhi, Trinity, and Malachi).

A special I love you to all my children (those I gave birth to and to those I did not).

Contents

What are the 3 main values a child should learn:

1. Self-Respect
2. Respect of Others
3. Voice Control

Definitions:

1. Self-Respect is defined as holding yourself in self-esteem and believing that you are good and worthy of being treated well.
2. Respect of Others is defined as someone or something elicited by their abilities, qualities or achievements.
3. Voice Control is defined as the power to direct your voice to influence behavior whether good or bad.

Introduction

As children there are three things that are very important in life. These three things will carry you a long way in life. Honor your mother and your father that your days may be long upon the earth. There are several things that I would like to include that applies to your every day life for a least eight hours in the day; respect and listen to your teachers because they are here to help you learn skills that you will need later in life. You see, teachers play a very important role in your growth process along with your parent(s). The three main things that people will remember about a person is how they respect themselves, how they respect others and the way they communicate with others.

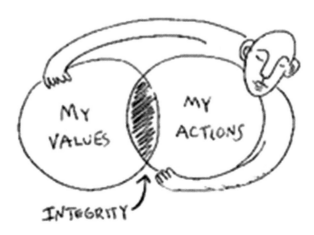

Encouragement

To the teachers, I commend you on the job you do daily in instructing the students and encouraging them to excel in what they do as a learning tool. We all know that education is very important and for you to do it with smiles on your face is so awesome. I want to take this time to say thank you for all your hard work and dedication. You all are special and know that someone is in your corner sending up prayers for you daily.

To the children, I encourage you to listen, do as requested, and stay out of the principles office. Your education is very important. You cannot learn the skills you need being absent from school on something that can be prevented, parent(s) have to work so that they can provide you with the necessities that you need(food, clothing, roof over your head, lights) they cannot do this if they have to miss work because you made the decision to misbehave at school. Education is fun, and you can learn great things. Apply yourself, because you have the potential to be who you desire to be, for example, if you desire to become a basketball player, you can do that. You do not have to be a statistic in the system of life, but you can be a helper in life. Make wise choices because every choice comes with a consequence.

Self-Respect

Self-Respect is to love yourself. When you do not love yourself, you cannot love others.

Your actions will show how you love yourself, so be mindful of your behavior. Always know that someone is watching you at all times in the classroom, hallway, bathroom, lunchroom, gym, and bus-room. Keep in mind that your first impression is a lasting impression. For example, if you always have a frown on your face, then people will perceive or think that you are mad or sad. I encourage you have a good day even when you are not having such a good day. Self-respect consist of taking care of yourself, by not staying up late on a school night especially when you know you have a test the next day. A tired mind cannot give its best, which means trouble on the horizon (you will be frustrated because you want to sleep and cannot sleep) school is a place to learn not sleep unless you are in preschool. Self-respect also consist of grooming yourself, by being presentable (taking the time to prepare the night before (after homework is complete).

Something to think about:

If you do not respect or love yourself, then others will not love and respect you. How you present yourself is how others will see you, for example, if your hair is not combed and your clothes are not ironed, then people will talk about you in a very negative way. In other words, you are the best representation of you.

Respect of Others

Respecting others is a sure sign that you respect yourself. There is no need to be jealous of someone else because they work or learn differently from you. You all are getting the same type of education.

Respect of others carries a lot of weight, for example, when you say yes ma'am, no ma'am, yes sir no sir, it shows that you respect not only yourself but others also. Respect is earned not given, you treat people the way you want to be treated and others will treat you likewise. We all know the golden rule: do unto others as you would have them do unto you. If you lie on others instead of telling the truth, others will lie on you instead of telling the truth. When the teacher asks you, what happened in a situation, if you do not know, then say I do not know (do not make something up). Respect of others goes something like this: (standing in line) …. John Wayne is standing behind Sally Mae and Sally Mae turns around and hit John Wayne for poking her in the side. So, the teacher asks you what happen, but you did not see it. What will you do? Will you make something up or will you say I did not see it? John Wayne disrespected Sally Mae because Sally Mae was standing quietly in line waiting for instructions from the teacher. It is very important to respect one another line space, this will keep you out of trouble. Respecting others while in class, means that you do not talk out of turn (bursting out), but you let the individual finish and if you have something to say (raise your hand) when the teacher acknowledge you, then you speak. Talking while others are talking is very rude and disrespectful (let them finish first). When you disrupt the class while the teacher is teaching that is very disrespectful. Talking back to your teachers in a negative way is disrespectful. Do not get an attitude if the teacher asks you a question, if you do not know the answer, just say I do not know, and the teacher will help you find the answer. Remember, you are learning to do the work.

 # Something to think about:

How would you feel if you were talking and someone just started talking? A). Would you feel mad? B.) Would you feel happy? C). Would you feel disrespected? D). Walk out the room?

Voice Control

When you speak in a respectable manner; the response will be in a respectable manner. Talking in a disrespectable manner is showing that you do not respect yourself or the person you are communicating with.

Your voice determines the outcome, for example, if the teacher takes you outside of the classroom to talk to you about your behavior, you are given time to cool off. Take that moment to quickly think about what you did. Take a deep breath and apologize for what you did. Answer any question that the teacher asks and always remember you are at school to learn and not disrupt the class because of something you do not understand. If you do not understand then raise your hand and ask the teacher a question (once the teacher acknowledge your hand raised). Back to using your inside voice and not your outside voice, your inside voice means you are talking in a respectable manner, your outside voice (when mad) only brings problems that will cause you to either be sent to the principles office and then sent home. Always use your inside voice (respectable) when talking to your teacher, parent(s), or someone older than you. They key to it all is to communicate in a respectable way. What you do in school now will affect you later. Get your education, respect others, do your homework (make sure to turn it in on time). Listen to your parent(s), if something is going on with you (education wise) or something you do not understand, raise your hand and talk to your teacher. Just a friendly reminder: your tone(voice) determines the outcome of any situation. For example, if you have anger in your voice while talking to the teacher, parent(s) or police, you are only hurting yourself (office referral, suspension from school, parent(s) missing work, juvenile record). Make wise choices with your voice by talking with respect and not disrespect. You are a reflection or representation of you, whether good or bad.

 # **Something to think about:**

What do you want to be when you grow up?

A). Teacher B). Football player C). Basketball Player D). Doctor E). Lawyer F). Other

You can be what you desire to be, but you must apply yourself, get good grades, communicate(calmly). Trust your teachers, because they may have been teaching way longer than you have been born (learn out loud). It is up to you to get your education. Learn all you can and then apply what you have learned.

 Teachers are a gift from God to help you as children learn skills that will help you later in life. Always remember, education is very important.

 Learning is fun when you are focused on the task at hand and not being disruptive in class. So, I encourage you to learn, learn, learn, and learn some more.

Applying what you learn daily is a skill that will help you to move forward. Always remain humble and teachable because you are never to old learn. Learning is something that will continue throughout your life.

Listen to one another and do not interrupt your fellow classmate, raise your hand, and wait to be acknowledge by your teacher.

One more important value while getting your education, PAY ATTENTION!!! YOU WILL BE TESTED ON WHAT YOU HAVE LEARNED IN CLASS AND YOUR GRADES WILL REVEAL TO THE TEACHER AND YOUR PARENTS IF YOU STUDIED FOR THE TEST. There is only one test that you cannot prepare for and that is a POP QUIZ, so it is vital that you PAY ATTENTION IN CLASS.

Team work gets things done!!! So work together so that everyone is successful in class and in life. Remember there are no I's and U's in team.

Unity is the key for success, while communicating with your teacher. So when its time to work as a team be awesome in it. All your gifts work together to help each other.

A special pledge for your
success:

I pledge to respect others.

I pledge to respect myself.

I pledge to listen to my teacher.

I pledge to use my inside voice.

I pledge to do my homework.

I pledge to turn my homework in on time.

I pledge to help my fellow classmates if they are struggling.

I pledge not to help my classmates cheat on test.

I pledge to study for tests given by the teacher.

I pledge to lead by example.

I pledge to communicate with others respectably.

I pledge to raise my hand when I have a question.

I pledge to stay in the classroom and not in the principle's office.

Printed in the United States
By Bookmasters